REAL WORLD ECONOMICS™

How Markets Work

Diane Bailey

ROSEN
PUBLISHING®
New York

Published in 2012 by The Rosen Publishing Group, Inc.
29 East 21st Street, New York, NY 10010

First Edition

Library of Congress Cataloging-in-Publication Data

Bailey, Diane, 1966-
How markets work/Diane Bailey.—1st ed.
        p. cm.—(Real world economics)
Includes bibliographical references and index.
ISBN 978-1-4488-5564-3 (library binding)
1. Capitalism—Juvenile literature.
2. Free enterprise—Juvenile literature.
3. Markets—Juvenile literature. I. Title.
HB501.B2247 2012
381—dc23

2011017462

Manufactured in China

CPSIA Compliance Information: Batch #W12YA: For further information, contact Rosen Publishing, New York, New York, at
1-800-237-9932.

On the cover: The volatile nature of the stock market can lead to some stress-inducing newspaper headlines.

Contents

INTRODUCTION

As high-tech cell phones go, Apple's iPhone is at the top. Not only is it a phone, it also offers an Internet connection, a music player, and hundreds of applications, or apps, from playing games to making your phone into a flashlight. All this doesn't come cheap. The iPhone costs hundreds of dollars. However, many customers are willing to pay the price. They'll even line up to get it! The demand for iPhones is big, and Apple has successfully cornered the market.

Most iPhone users live in the United States, but the phone itself is the product of many global markets. The technology was developed in the United States. Some of the parts are also made in America, while others are made in other countries. Then, the phone is assembled in China.

By using parts and labor located outside the United States, Apple has been criticized for being greedy and trying to get more profits at the expense of U.S. workers. Two researchers wrote a report saying the iPhone had added almost $2 billion to the U.S. trade deficit (the amount that imports exceed exports). They also said Apple could manufacture the phones in the United States and still make a big profit.

That move might be good for some U.S. workers. However, in today's world, the idea of a market economy is not just national, but global. Even if something is bad for U.S. workers, it could be good for Chinese workers, for example. And outsourcing—using materials and labor from other areas—isn't necessarily bad. For example, by hiring inexpensive labor, Apple could save money that it then can reinvest in developing technology. That would mean jobs for U.S. workers.

All these factors working together make market economies complex systems, but the basic idea is simple. A market economy is driven by what products or services are available (the supply) and how much people want them (the demand). Based on these factors, prices are determined. If enough buyers want something badly enough—like an iPhone—the price can be

Apple's iPhone is extremely popular in the United States and around the world, allowing Apple to capture a large market share of the high-end cellular phone business.

high. On the other hand, if a seller wants to get rid of something, he or she will have to lower the price to attract buyers.

In a market economy, buyers have a choice about what they purchase—and from whom. Sellers can decide the best way to make and promote their products. Both sides are always looking for the best deal. This creates competition. In general, having people compete against one another leads everyone to do the best they can.

Coke or Pepsi? Pens or pencils? Every time you make a decision to buy something, you are participating in a market economy. Although your choice might be easy for you, there are many factors at work that you don't see. People make millions of choices every day. Some are small; some are big. Add them all up, and together they create and drive the market economy.

CHAPTER ONE

APPLES FOR ORANGES

Some people like to "shop 'til they drop." Others like it when things go a little more quickly. Fortunately for both kinds of people, market economies are the best way to go! Variety and bargains are all results of a market economy.

What Makes a Market?

You want it? We got it! A market has a few basic parts. First, there must be a supplier—someone to provide goods or services. These can be anything from computers to clothes to cable TV service. Next, there must be someone who wants to acquire these products, either by buying them or trading for them.

But there's a third element in a market. Suppose you are sitting with a friend at lunch, and you agree to trade your granola bar for her chocolate chip cookies. This isn't really a market because it's missing an important component: choice. In a true market environment, people have the choice to buy from someone else.

A customer eyes the merchandise displayed in the window of an American Apparel store in Washington, D.C. The company features casual clothing that is made entirely in the United States.

Now suppose a third friend is at this lunch table. She's got a bag of potato chips she doesn't want, but she does want your granola bar. Now a market has been created. You have the option of trading your granola bar for either potato chips or cookies. And your friends have the option of trading with each other—chips for cookies—and leaving you out of the loop altogether. Add in a few more friends with lunch boxes full of peanut butter and jelly sandwiches and pudding cups, and you've got the "ingredients" for a busy market.

Most of the world's countries use some form of a market economy—although it's a lot more complicated than what kind of crumbs end up in your lap!

9

Command Economies

Market economies are the most common, efficient, and powerful types of economies. However, they are not the only kind. In a planned economy, also called a command economy, a government controls what is produced, how much is produced, and how much things cost. These types of economies are common in socialist or communist countries, where governments try to make things fair for everyone by controlling the economy. However, a market economy usually does a better job of this by itself than when government gets involved. Also, even if a government could effectively control prices and wages, it doesn't take into account the fact that people like having choices.

TYPES OF MARKETS

Many things are sold in market environments. The most obvious one is the market for actual things (called goods) like food, clothing, cars, houses, and all the other stuff people buy. Services include anything from getting a haircut to taking a taxi ride. Getting a college education would also be a type of service—although students will also have to buy goods like books.

Some things are sold on exchanges. An exchange is a group or organization that makes it easier to buy and sell by creating a common environment for buyers and sellers. Basic materials like wheat, oil, and iron are called commodities. These are sold on exchanges. So are financial products like stocks and bonds.

A college student waits to purchase an armful of textbooks. Not all students buy books new; there are also markets for used books and electronic books.

Labor is another market. No goods or services get made if someone doesn't make them. That's where workers come in. A person's skills, education, and ability to work will determine how he or she can compete in the labor market. How desirable a job is, and how much it pays, will affect a company's ability to attract workers.

There's even a market for markets. Specialized markets—or niches—are important to the economy. For example, the "green market" refers to products and services that involve the environment. These could include eco-friendly toilet paper or a service to clean up toxic waste. The black market is more sinister. This refers to the market for dealing in goods or services illegally. It could be that the product itself is illegal, such as drugs. Or it could mean that although the item itself is legal, the seller can make more money or the buyer can pay less (or both) if they make a deal without going through the proper channels. For example, someone might steal a bunch of televisions and sell them on the street corner for much less than they would cost at a store.

SUPPLY AND DEMAND

Market economies operate on a basic idea called the law of supply and demand. A seller supplies products or services to a buyer. The buyer creates the demand for the product. Of course, a market has many sellers and buyers. Each one has different priorities and resources.

Perhaps the most obvious factor at work in a market environment is price. How much is a buyer willing to pay in order to feel that he's gotten his money's worth? How much is a seller willing to take in order to feel that she's covered her costs and gotten a little extra—profit—for her work? Neither player will go through with the deal if they don't feel like they are getting something out of it.

Let's say it costs a seller $.40 to make a candy bar. He'd like to sell it for $.75 and make $.35 in profit. Now let's say we've got a hungry buyer. She's budgeted $1 for her snack, so she could afford to pay the $.75 the seller wants. However, she's going to be thirsty as well, so she's hoping to hold back $.40 for a cup of lemonade. Therefore, she offers to pay $.60 for the candy bar. The seller is not making as much as he'd hoped, but it's still a decent profit. A deal is struck.

Signs at the retail giant Walmart advertise the store's low prices. Some people criticize the company, saying that bargain prices mean that workers and manufacturers are paid poorly.

Of course, in a market there are more than two people involved. The seller may have discovered that no one is willing to pay him $.75 for his candy bar because another seller is offering them for less. The buyer, for her part, finds out that no candy bar costs less than $.50 because then the sellers won't make enough profit. Over time, and throughout the market, the requirements for the buyer and seller start to even out. This is called equilibrium. The result—a candy bar costs $.60—is called the market clearing price.

However, this does not mean every candy bar always costs $.60. Other things may influence the price. For example, at the only gas station for a stretch of many miles, a candy bar will probably cost more. For one thing, it costs the store owner more to get the candy bars there in the first place. He will have to factor that into his price. The buyer, on the other hand, won't have the opportunity to buy a candy bar for a while. So she's willing to pay more. The market clearing price depends on all the factors at work.

Deal or No Deal?

When you go to the store, you look at the price of an item and then decide whether you want to buy it. If it's a good deal, you'll take it. If you think you can do better somewhere else, you might shop around. In the United States, most consumers aren't used to negotiating directly with a seller. If they don't like the price or terms of a sale, they'll simply go elsewhere. However, in other countries, merchants often expect their customers to haggle—try to get a lower price. The seller will ask a high price, and the customer will counter with something lower. Then they will negotiate back and forth until they arrive at a place in the middle that they both agree on.

SURPLUS AND SHORTAGE

Other factors besides price are at work in a market economy. For example, maybe a buyer prefers the product of one seller, but knows he will have to drive all the way across town to get it. Or perhaps the buyer needs it in a hurry, but most sellers can't deliver for another month. All of these things will affect the choice the buyer actually makes. Driving across town will

A corn farmer in Iowa examines the condition of his crop. Although a bumper crop—meaning a large yield—might offer sizable profits, the increased supply can also drive prices down.

cost him time and gas money. Waiting might not be an option for him. All of these factors will influence the final decision.

One consideration is availability. When there's more of something than people want, it's called a surplus. This drives the price down. On the other hand, when there's not enough to meet the demand, there's a shortage, and it drives the price up. For example, suppose the farmers in an area produce a lot of corn one year. It would seem that because they have more to sell, they will make more money. However, there is only so much corn people are going to eat. The supply is greater than the demand. In order for the farmers to sell their corn, they may have to offer it at a lower price to attract buyers.

The reverse is also true. If there's hardly any corn, buyers will be scrambling to find some. When they do, they might snatch it up at a higher price to ensure that they get it before someone else does.

In this scenario, someone might not get any corn. He's going to have to eat beans instead. This does not mean that the market system didn't work. Instead, it means the buyer made a choice based on his preferences (what he likes to eat), his resources (how much money he has), and the availability (the amount of corn that's for sale). Even if he likes corn better, he may be able to buy twice as many beans and get more to eat in the long run. What he lost in preference, he made up for in amount.

CHAPTER TWO

DRIVING FORCES

I magine that you live ten thousand years ago. Your tribe lives on a hillside and grows berries. Over the years, the people in your tribe have learned how to plant, care for, and harvest berries so that they get the most they can out of the available growing space. However, when it comes to hunting rabbits, your people have a lot more trouble. Their bows and arrows break all the time, and their aim is terrible. A few miles away, however, lives another tribe. They are great hunters, but hopeless at growing berries. What's more, they're sick of only eating rabbits, and you're sick of only eating berries.

Anyone up for a trade?

Everybody Wins

People need a variety of things. After all, no one is going to survive on berries (or rabbits) alone. In the past, people were more self-sufficient. Our tribal ancestors, for example, probably

17

could hunt rabbits if they had to. However, they were better at growing berries, and they liked it more. By creating an environment to buy, sell, and trade goods—a market—people give themselves the ability to specialize.

If our berry-growers knew they could trade berries for rabbits, they could focus on growing berries and not worry about where the rabbits were coming from. As they devoted their time to growing berries, they got better and more efficient. They could grow more. In general, when people produce more of something, they can do it faster and for less money. This is called economy of scale. In addition, when people specialize, markets are created for things that aren't strictly necessary. Our ancestors may have had a third tribe busy making dishes for the feast.

In this sixteenth-century artwork, Native Americans are depicted working the fields in Florida. Early agricultural workers learned the best crops to grow for their environments—and the most efficient ways to raise them.

A theory called zero-sum states that in a situation where one party gains something, another must lose the same amount. For example, if you are playing Monopoly and charge your opponent $25 rent, she loses that $25. You can't both have it.

A market, however, is more like a positive-sum game. In this scenario, think of two countries that are trading with one another. Perhaps the United States is selling popular music CDs to Brazil. Brazil, in turn, is selling coffee to Americans. The price of the CDs and the coffee might balance out, but each country feels like it is coming out ahead because it is getting a product it could not get otherwise. In addition, the process of making and exporting those products creates jobs for people. This is a positive-sum game.

"I, Pencil"

In 1958, Leonard Read wrote an essay called "I, Pencil." It told the "life story" of a pencil, and how it had been made with a combination of different materials, using the skills of a number of different people. From the graphite (lead) in the pencil, to its wooden exterior, to the eraser, the expertise of many people was needed to make even such a simple product as a pencil. With the story, Read showed how market economies depend on specialization and cooperation. The piece also argues against the idea of a planned economy, since no one person or institution can deal with every factor that goes into making a product—not even something as simple as a pencil. One college professor called the essay "a superb case study of free markets in action." He added, "Half of the world's economic problems would vanish if everyone would read 'I, Pencil.'"

THE INTRODUCTION OF MONEY

Trading apples for oranges (or chips for cookies) is a form of direct trade called barter. This is one of the oldest ways to exchange goods, but it is not the easiest. When many people are involved, it can get confusing. One person might want oranges, but only has cookies to trade. The person who has oranges to trade is not interested in cookies. She wants honey-roasted peanuts. Unfortunately, the person who has those isn't hungry at all. He wants a new shirt. All these people have things to trade, but it's hard to get organized enough to make it work.

Enter money.

Money, or currency, is used to represent other things. The paper it's printed on is not useful by itself. It can't be eaten or worn, for example. However, the people who use it all agree to give it a value. Now, instead of having to trade one item for another item, everyone can use the same money. In 1999, several countries in Europe agreed to stop using their individual currencies and cooperate by using one called the euro. Because European nations did most of their trade with each other, having a common currency reduced trade problems caused by different exchange rates and different political agendas.

A young man checks his wallet. Money, or currency, makes the exchange of goods and services much easier because people agree to use it as a common basis for trade.

Money to Burn

During World War II, prisoners living at a camp received rations from the Red Cross. These were packages with items such as chocolate, sugar, butter, and cigarettes. The prisoners developed a complex barter system in order to trade items. Over time, cigarettes, which were one of the most desirable items, became a form of money. The price of items was expressed as a certain number of cigarettes. For example, a ration of cheese might cost seven cigarettes. Some entrepreneurs created market niches, such as setting up coffee stands where they brewed and sold coffee for two cigarettes a cup. In keeping with the laws of supply and demand, when the supply of cigarettes was running low, prices would fall. They would rise again after a new shipment of cigarettes came in. Not all cigarettes were the same: in this unique economy, people used the low-quality cigarettes for money, but they smoked the high-quality ones.

When things are expensive, it's tempting to wish that the government would simply print more money. Unfortunately, that would not work. If people had more money to spend, they would be in a position to offer higher prices to buy goods—and sellers would be able to ask for more money. The competition would still be the same; it would just be happening at a higher price level.

Markets developed because they offered more to the participants than they could achieve acting only on their own. Money was developed because it made it easier to act in the marketplace. It's the ultimate app!

THE MARKET FOR MONEY

Just as there are markets for food, clothing, and other products, there is also a market for money itself. Banks, credit companies, and the stock market are all places where money can be bought and sold.

You have to spend money to make money. Any business owner is familiar with that concept. However, since it's difficult to find enough spare change laying on the ground to invest in a business, people have had to find other ways. They need capital—money that can be spent to grow a business.

Let's return to our berry-growing tribe and fast-forward them a few thousand years. They're still picking berries, but now they want to branch out into making jam. To do this, they're going to need to purchase equipment. Waiting for their small profits to add up would take too long, so they look for other ways to get money faster. One possibility is going to the bank and getting a loan. When a bank makes a loan, it charges interest. The borrower agrees to pay the money back, plus some extra. For that extra money, the bank is selling the opportunity to have the money sooner. In the case of the berry-growers, they are betting that they will sell so much jam that they will be able to cover the cost of paying the money back and still make a profit.

If a company gets even larger—or needs a lot of money—the stock market may come in. A share of stock in a company is basically a small piece of it. A company can sell shares to investors in order to raise money to grow the company.

When an investor buys stock in a company, he or she then owns a percentage of it. If the company makes money, it might pay the stockholder a bonus called a dividend. Or it

Financial markets are driven by banks and investment firms, which make loans to individuals and companies and are involved with issuing stocks and bonds.

might reinvest profits in the company to help it grow. If it is a successful company, its worth will go up, and that will make the price of the stock go up. (Of course, the reverse might happen as well—that's why the stock market is a gamble.)

Bonds are another way that the financial markets create money for the economy. Essentially, a bond is a very large loan. A bond is usually issued by a government agency that is borrowing the money. All the investors who buy into the bond are the lenders.

Today, there is a large, sophisticated system just for financial markets. Money may not make the world go 'round, but it does grease the wheels!

MYTHS and FACTS

MYTH All products and services should be offered in a free market economy.

FACT Some shared resources, such as roads or providing military defense, often work better when regulated by a government.

MYTH Buying domestic products is the best way to save jobs.

FACT Increased trade between countries spurs competition, increases the buying power of developing nations, and can help create more domestic jobs as people find new markets.

MYTH Market economies often don't leave room for the "little guy" to compete.

FACT Countries with less-developed economies can do well in a market environment because they can provide goods and services at a discount.

CHAPTER THREE

MARKETS AT WORK

For a market economy to work, the participants all have to feel like they are getting something out of it. Otherwise, they would not do it. But everyone has different priorities and different goals. They do not have the same amounts of money, information, or other resources. So how can all these people work together? There's a simple answer: they don't have to.

The Invisible Hand

In the 1700s, the economist Adam Smith wrote about an "invisible hand" that helped guide market economies. People who participate in a market will obviously make decisions they believe will help them. However, even when people are acting for themselves, those actions do not necessarily have a negative effect on someone else. In *The Wealth of Nations*, published in 1776, Smith wrote, "By pursuing his own interest [a businessman] frequently promotes that of the society more effectually than when he really intends to promote it."

What's the trick? By acting for his own benefit, a person is guided to behavior that helps himself. However, that behavior often helps others as well. For example, to succeed in a marketplace, a seller must find efficient ways to make his product. He will probably look for good prices on materials. He will want workers who are effective. Those actions are in his own self-interest because they will keep his costs down. Then he can offer his products at competitive prices. That, in turn, helps the buyers, who now can pay less.

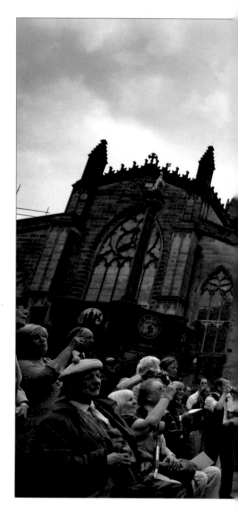

The buyer has a part in this cycle, too. Rather than just accept whatever the seller wants, most buyers will refuse to pay too much. That ensures the seller stays efficient. Each person's behavior is affecting the whole process.

MOVERS AND MOTIVATORS

The "invisible hand" has a lot of fingers because markets are guided by several factors. There are the quantity, quality, and variety of products available. Then there's the willingness of consumers to buy those products. That is determined by their needs, wants, and how much money they have to spend. Supply and demand are the building blocks of a market economy. These are constantly shifting. Companies develop new products or improve old ones, and customers come up with new things that they want.

A bronze statue of Adam Smith was unveiled in 2008 in Edinburgh, Scotland, the city where the eighteenth-century philosopher and economist worked. Smith remains famous today for his theories.

Incentives are a big part of how markets function. A seller wants to make money, so her incentive is profit. Of course, she could fail at her business and lose money, so she is taking a risk as well. But if she's in business in the first place, she expects a return—profit—that will outweigh the risks. To maximize her chances of succeeding, this businessperson will now need to be competitive. She's got to offer a product that fulfills some need or want for her buyers. It can't be so expensive that her target customers can't afford it, but it can't be so cheap that she does not make any money. She has to make sure her products are desirable, available, and affordable. The item does not have to be the best in all three categories. It just has to have the right combination to make it attractive to a certain amount of buyers.

Suppose a merchant offers a product that's similar to what another seller has available. However, it's not exactly the same. It's different enough that it will appeal to a specific type of buyer. By developing a market niche like this, a seller can stay competitive. For example, maybe two manufacturers are both selling a camera that costs $150. It's not the same camera, though. One of them has a zoom lens, whereas the other one has a fixed lens. The one with the fixed lens, however, is smaller and easier to carry around.

Because different customers have different preferences, both sellers can compete in the marketplace. Now a third manufacturer enters the picture. It's got a camera that is both small and has a zoom lens. With both advantages, this company

Customers examine digital cameras at a store in Pennsylvania. By selling products that offer different features at different prices, companies can target a specific customer base and gain market share.

can sell its camera for $200. It will attract buyers who want a fancier camera and are willing to spend the money to get it.

As these three companies compete for customers, consumers benefit as well. They have more choices and are more likely to find a camera that suits their preferences and their budgets.

Thinking Outside of the Box

Most children know the Slinky and Silly Putty as toys, but neither of them began that way. Instead, both were invented when researchers were trying to develop products that were needed during World War II. The Slinky evolved from work being done with springs that were needed to stabilize items on ships. Silly Putty was the result of trying to find a replacement for rubber, which was difficult to get during the war. Neither product ended up being helpful for the war, but both became hugely popular toys, thanks to people who recognized that they could fill a different market niche. This process of innovation, and finding how it has economic value, is an important element in driving market economies.

Other Factors

Besides the quality of an item and its price, consumers are influenced by other factors that also affect the market for a product. For example, suppose there are two companies that make blue jeans. One of them provides well-made jeans

Dark, stonewashed, ripped, embroidered: the choices for a pair of jeans are practically endless. Brand names—and the reputations they bring with them—also affect customers' eventual decisions.

using sturdy fabric and offers them for $25 a pair. The other makes jeans of equal quality, but they cost $50. However, this second company is selling a designer brand that appeals to people who want the status that comes with wearing designer jeans.

A customer might also choose to go with a known brand because he believes it will be reliable. He has some idea what he's getting. Someone going out to dinner in an unfamiliar town might choose to eat at a chain restaurant that he knows from his hometown. Even if the food is more expensive, he can depend on it to be close to what he would get at home.

Customers might also choose to buy something that costs more because they feel they are doing something good in the process. For example, recycled paper costs more than regular paper. Even though a buyer is not getting any more value from the actual product, she is "buying" the value of preserving the

environment. Someone might also choose to buy clothing from a company that guarantees its workers are treated well and paid fairly. Here, the consumer is making a choice based on his standards for being socially responsible.

The New York Stock Exchange, located on Wall Street, operates in conjunction with Europe's Euronext as the largest stock exchange in the world. The two merged in 2007.

INFLUENCE OF TECHNOLOGY

Bananas might be nature's "most perfect food," but it took a little more work to make them into a marketable import to America. In 1871, an American businessman began building a railroad in the Central American country of Costa Rica. He planted banana trees beside the tracks. This made it easy for the bananas to be taken to ships that could bring them to the United States. Thanks to improved transportation technology, a market was created for something that would otherwise have been unavailable. Increased technology has also taken away the market for certain goods. For example, no one buys typewriters anymore—they buy computers.

More recently, information technology has exploded. Books, newspapers, magazines, and television spread information to people, influencing their choices of what to buy. The Internet takes that several steps further. It takes virtually no effort to comparison shop online, forcing suppliers to be even more competitive.

It's also created opportunities for smaller companies with specialty products. They might not otherwise have the ability to reach a large number of people. With the Internet, it is easier to find a market for uncommon items. For example, somebody, somewhere, might want a pair of $100 handcrafted mittens made from duck feathers and scented to smell like raspberries. Most people will still buy their mittens at a local store, but the Internet helps support the "choice" element of a market economy.

The Internet also gets around two huge problems of delivering information: speed and distance. A physical object can't be immediately transported across the world, but information can. An e-mail takes only a second to go from Florida to France. Of course, it was possible to exchange information globally before, but the Internet raised the stakes. Getting information is now faster, easier, and cheaper than ever before.

Not only did the Internet create new markets, it also changed how existing ones operate. One example is in the financial markets. It used to be that selling stocks and bonds happened at certain times, at a physical location such as the New York Stock Exchange (NYSE). Today, however, many trades are done online. There does not even have to be a person involved. Computers store the necessary information and then automatically carry out the transactions. This has led to an increased amount, or volume, of trading. Investors can react quickly to things they think will change the value of their investments.

CHAPTER FOUR
THE WORLDWIDE STAGE

In the 1989 movie *Field of Dreams*, a character wants to build a baseball field in the middle of nowhere to attract a long-dead baseball player. An invisible voice tells him, "If you build it, he will come." Indeed, the character builds the field, and not only does the baseball player show up, so does a whole team!

The same phenomenon is at work with markets. In a market economy, entrepreneurs can create markets that then attract customers. Remember the bananas? In addition, in a world that is increasingly connected through technology, markets have gone global. The workings of markets across the world all influence one another.

EMERGING MARKETS

The two main participants in a market—buyer and seller—do not necessarily have to be in the same place. To produce

38

goods or services, a business depends on the natural and human resources available. However, these things can be located separately—sometimes thousands of miles away—from the final consumer.

This gives flexibility to companies that might want to build a manufacturing plant in a foreign country, for example. For a buyer, it means access to a larger variety of things. It might be exotic foods that must be shipped over long distances. Or it might be a product that would be too expensive for an average person if it had not been made using labor that did not cost as much.

Emerging markets are ones that are still developing. They are often able to get a foothold by offering advantages like inexpensive labor. Of course, some people object to using cheap labor from foreign countries. They believe it takes jobs away from local workers, and that sometimes the foreign workers are

Big Business in a Small Package

Hong Kong is a small part of China, but a lot of people live there. It is one of the most densely populated places in the world. Hong Kong does not have that many natural resources. There is not enough space to operate large farms, for example. Despite its small size, Hong Kong has a powerhouse economy. It has made good use of what it does have—people. Workers there are well-educated and able to compete in the global market for information. The region has developed a strong financial industry. In addition, there are low taxes, and trade with other countries is easy.

not treated well. Nonetheless, markets require companies to be competitive. It's no surprise that they look for every advantage they can find. It can also help the people who do get the jobs because it gives them increased buying power.

Corporations take advantage of India's inexpensive labor force to provide telephone support to customers in the United States and other parts of the world.

Compared to many other countries, labor in India is inexpensive. To take advantage of this, some companies have put call centers there. Workers provide telephone support to customers who live in other parts of the world. This makes economic

sense for the company hiring the workers. It also provides jobs for people in India, which helps the country compete in the global economy.

Emerging markets might also have something called comparative advantage. This means that even if they can't do something better, they can do it well enough that it makes sense to give them the work. For example, suppose you and a friend decide to start a business washing cars. You're a little bit better at washing the cars than your friend. However, you're much better at finding customers. But you can't do both. You need your friend's help. He has a comparative advantage in washing the cars. Even though he's not quite as good as you, if you compare the two parts of the business it makes sense for you to spend your time promoting the business and for him to take over the washing. Then you can both make more money!

It works the same with global markets. A developed country might do two things better than an emerging country, but it makes sense to let the growing country take over one of the responsibilities. That way, the developed country can focus on what it does much better.

Going Global

Global trade is not a new idea. It has increased as technology has advanced and people have become more aware of opportunities. However, some people still resist the idea of importing cheaper products or using cheaper labor from other countries.

An economic approach called mercantilism argues that if countries can export (sell) more than they import (buy), they will make more money and raise the standard of living for

their citizens. It sounds like a good idea, but in practice it does not quite work. For one thing, if there is a lot of money being made from imports, prices are going to go up. We have seen that with the law of supply and demand. Also, the rest of the

President John F. Kennedy speaks to the press during the 1962 Cuban Missile Crisis. In the months leading up to the standoff, America imposed an embargo on Cuba to protest its political operations.

world will probably get tired of this kid who won't play nice on the playground. If this country will not buy from others, why should others buy from it?

Staying self-sufficient (or trying to) is not always a good plan. This goes for countries as well as individuals. When countries trade with one another, they can specialize in what they do best and become more efficient participants in the global market. Certainly, some people will lose. Workers may suffer as they are downsized and their jobs move overseas. There is no denying that this can be painful for the families involved. But to take a more global view, the people who get the jobs will benefit.

Who's Going to Settle This?

With about 150 countries trading with each other, there are bound to be some disagreements. That's where the World Trade Organization (WTO) comes in. The WTO was created in 1994 so that its member countries would have a place where they could work out trade problems. To be a member of the WTO, a country's government agrees to follow the recommendations a WTO committee makes. Through negotiations, the WTO works to make global trade easier and open up trade markets to emerging economies. However, in some cases, the WTO supports stricter trade barriers if it decides that open trade would somehow hurt consumers. An example would be if trade would contribute to spreading disease. A big part of the WTO's job is to make things fair for the parties involved. This is where things get tricky, since one country's idea of "fair" isn't always the same as another's!

Of course, countries want to encourage their domestic industries. They can try to give a "home field advantage" without actually closing the doors to international trade. To do this, they might try to even the playing field by imposing taxes (called tariffs) on imported goods. This makes the products more expensive, but they are still available. Another strategy is to have quotas, meaning that only a certain amount of something is allowed to enter the country. When the supply is limited, it will drive the price up. Some people will have to turn elsewhere.

Occasionally, a country will put an embargo on imports from another country. An embargo means that something is prohibited from being traded. This is usually done to make a political point. For example, most products from Cuba—including its famous cigars—are illegal in the United States. It's been that way for almost fifty years. The United States closed off the market to Cuba in 1962 to protest its communist government and violations of human rights. In January 2011, President Barack Obama eased the embargo, allowing Americans to travel there.

NEGATIVE SIDE EFFECTS

No system is perfect, of course. Markets are influenced by more than just what's for sale and at what price. Politics plays a part. Major world events, like wars or natural disasters, all affect the economic markets. So do social factors like race and religion. In an unbiased system, the best products from the most competitive sellers would always win. However, personal prejudices sometimes get in the way.

Another problem arises when people share resources. If everyone only used their own money and their own property, their decisions would only affect them. However, that is not always the case. In 1968, a Texas ecologist named Garrett Hardin wrote an essay called "The Tragedy of the Commons." In it, he used an example raised in the 1800s by a British writer who showed that when people are acting in their immediate self-interest, it can have a negative effect in the long run.

The example is about several herdsmen who graze their cattle on a shared piece of land. Each herdsman will do better individually if he can raise more cows because he gets the money when he sells his animals. In addition, he does not have much incentive to preserve the land because it does not belong to him. If he does not use it, someone else will. However, the land

When multiple people share a common resource—such as a field for cattle to graze in—it can be difficult to divide it fairly and preserve its value, as Garrett Hardin wrote in "The Tragedy of the Commons."

can only support so many animals. If it is overgrazed, there will be no grass left, and no one will be able to raise cows. Then, everyone loses out.

Today, this kind of situation could be applied to other environmental problems, such as pollution. A company might pollute the air or water when it manufactures its products. This is a cost to all of society. The polluting company might benefit for a while, but eventually it, too, will pay a higher price. It would seem Adam Smith's "invisible hand" only reaches so far.

CHAPTER FIVE

AN IMPERFECT SYSTEM

Market economies work well for things like mortgages and MP3 players. However, things get a little fuzzy when it comes to other things people need or want. Shared resources, such as the herdsmen's land, are difficult to regulate in a strict market economy. That's where governments come in. They get involved when they believe that a better outcome can be achieved by putting a limit on the free market.

THE MYTH OF THE FREE MARKET ECONOMY

A free market is one that functions only by the actions and decisions of the people involved, without any outside intervention. However, very few—if any—free markets actually exist. There is free and there is more free, but there is no absolutely free.

Some products and services can be distributed more effectively, and more fairly, when they are regulated by the

All citizens benefit from infrastructure such as roads and bridges, or community services such as police and fire service, so all citizens are required to help pay for them through taxes.

government and paid for by taxes. For example, everybody needs roads. However, it would be difficult to go around to everyone, ask them how much they plan to use the roads, and then charge them the appropriate amount. They may say they don't plan to use the roads at all, but if they're there, you can bet they will. Military, police, and fire service are other examples of shared resources that would be hard to divide up in a free market system. Other things are partly in the free market. Utilities like electricity, for example, may be supplied by several competing companies. However, these companies are usually heavily regulated by governments.

To take our pollution example from the previous chapter, suppose each person was asked to chip in to clean up the environment.

Illegal Activity

Successful markets depend on everyone doing what they're supposed to. Sometimes, however, people act illegally. In the stock market, traders can get in trouble for insider trading. When this happens, they are using information that most people don't have. For example, they might know that a company will soon make a lot of money because of a new product or discovery. The price of a company's stock would rise once this information became public. If a person knew in advance, he or she could buy the stock when it was still at a lower price. Another type of illegal activity is price fixing. In this scenario, two or more companies that offer similar products agree to sell at a certain price, taking away the competition between them and leaving customers with fewer choices.

Even people who refused to contribute would still benefit from the cleaner air and water, since it would be impossible to separate them. So, to make sure that everyone enjoys the benefit of these things—and helps pay for them—the government simply takes over. People are not completely excluded from the process. Through voting, they can help decide how much money will go to certain projects or services. However, they are only contributing to a collective choice, not making an individual one.

A well-known and sometimes controversial example is the U.S. Postal Service. If the post office operated in a free market, it might fail. Over the years, the government has helped it stay in business. According to federal law, no one else can deliver first-class mail in the United States. This law ensures that people in all parts of the United States can get reliable mail service at the same price as everyone else. However, many people have argued that mail delivery should be opened up to competitors.

The labor market is another example of a partly free market. It may be affected by minimum-wage laws or other laws that dictate who is allowed to work. In the United States, certain jobs are off-limits to people who are too young or who have a criminal record. Few people would argue that this is a bad idea, but it does show how the free market is being limited by the government.

Market Failure

An ideal market is efficient, meaning that resources are being used and distributed in the best way possible. Not everybody's definition of "best" is the same, of course. A seller wants more money, while a buyer wants to pay less. When a balance has been struck, however, the market is efficient because each participant is satisfied. The Italian economist Vilfredo Pareto explained a concept that is now called Pareto efficiency. It means that a market is at its most efficient when no participant can become better off without someone else becoming worse off. It doesn't mean everyone is getting exactly what they want. It means that the best compromise has been reached.

Nothing operates at complete efficiency, however. Things go off-kilter. The division of resources is not happening in the best way. For example, the supply of something does not equal demand. When this happens, it is called a market failure. "Failure" sounds really bad, but in reality, market failures often correct themselves.

A number of things can cause a market failure. Lack of information is one. For example, let's say a person is purchasing a home. The seller does not tell her the house needs a new roof, which will cost thousands of dollars. Without this information, the buyer may pay more than she would have if she had known the house had a major problem. In reality, there are laws against this. In theory, however, it could happen. The market failed because one person had more information than the other.

Another example is the minimum-wage law. In a free market, people would be paid based on their skills and how much labor was available. In a poor economy with fewer jobs, they might work for less money because they needed a job. In order to help people maintain a certain standard of living, however, a government could pass a minimum-wage law. Although this can help some people, it might be bad for others. Companies who only have so much money to spend would hire fewer workers. More people would be left without a job. In this case, it could be argued that market failure occurred.

However, there is no line drawn where one side is considered market success and the other market failure. It's often a gradual process. And one person's idea of failure might not be the same as another's.

A family receives the keys to their new home. The housing market is commonly looked at as an indicator of how well the overall economy is performing.

When Government Steps In

There's failure, and then there's failure. As a technical term, a market failure means a market is not operating at the best efficiency. In many cases, these failures correct themselves. Sometimes, however, things really go wrong. Then, it's usually up to a government to get involved.

Monopolies happen when one company controls the market for a given product or service. They are an example of a market failure. With no competition, a company has no incentive to be efficient. That may make its costs go up, and then consumers end up paying more. Or with no competition, the company could just decide to charge more because it knows people will have to pay it! Usually, the market for a particular product or service will spontaneously create competition, but occasionally things get out of balance. This is especially true with products or services that require specialized knowledge or large amounts of capital.

When telephone service was first introduced in the United States, it was controlled by the Bell System (named for Alexander Graham Bell, who invented the telephone). Bell was owned by AT&T. AT&T built and operated a huge network of telephone lines. It was nearly impossible for anyone else to break into the market.

Up until the 1970s, almost all U.S. phone service was handled by AT&T. Today, both cell phone and landline services are offered by many carriers, creating a competitive market.

In 1974, however, the U.S. government decided that AT&T had a monopoly. It thought consumers would be better served if there was competition for phone service. Antitrust laws rule against noncompetitive business practices, such as monopolies.

What's a Bubble?

When economists talk about market failures, they sometimes refer to "bubbles." If you think of water running through a tube, it should go in one end and out the other at a fairly constant rate. However, if there's a kink in the tube and the water gets stuck, it will expand the tube and cause a bubble. In markets, bubbles form when there's a kink in the market and a segment starts to artificially inflate. In the 2000s, U.S. home prices started increasing a lot—and fast. This created a bubble. The amounts of mortgages—the money people borrowed to pay for the houses—also went up. This, in turn, helped create the financial crisis of 2008, when it became clear that there was too much risk involved in many of the loans.

Using these laws, the government succeeded in breaking up AT&T into several smaller companies. This allowed other competitors into the market.

Governments may also get involved financially by providing subsidies. A subsidy is money given to individuals or companies to keep them from going broke. The free market is not at work here, but the idea is that the economy will be better off in the long run if the companies are not left to fail.

In some cases, subsidies may amount to a little boost. In other cases, it's a full-scale rescue. In 2008, the U.S. financial markets got into such serious trouble that the government took over to prevent the entire national system from failing.

Ten Great Questions
to Ask a Financial Adviser

1. What background and experience do you have?

2. How do you get paid? Is it through fees, commission, or some combination?

3. What services are you licensed to offer?

4. How often will we review my portfolio?

5. What is your investment philosophy?

6. How would you assess my financial situation?

7. What criteria will you use to decide if a particular investment is right for me?

8. What kinds of risk should I be thinking about given my age, income, and financial goals?

9. How will big changes in my life affect how I should change my investments?

10. What tax consequences will I be looking at for different investments?

CHAPTER SIX

MARKETS IN THE REAL WORLD

When you're healthy, you tend not to think much about it. It takes getting sick to realize how much better you felt when you were healthy. It's the same with markets. They are quiet things in general, making adjustments here and there when necessary, but generally not drawing attention to themselves. When they are functioning correctly, they don't get a lot of notice. It takes things going wrong to show what was going right.

THE CRASH OF 2008

When the U.S. financial markets crashed in 2008, it wasn't the first time. In 1929, the stock market crash led to the Great Depression, an economic downturn that lasted for years. In both cases, prices fell sharply as investors tried to sell stocks they believed were losing value—fast. Following the law of supply and demand, stocks got cheaper as there were more to buy and fewer people who wanted them. This fueled a panic. As prices fell, even more people wanted to get rid of their stocks. This drove prices even lower.

In 2008, the crash came after months of other extreme financial problems. For example, housing prices had been rising sharply in the last several years. To get people mortgages at these higher prices, banks were not being as careful as they normally would. They lent money to people who weren't able to pay it back. In the early months of 2008, it became clear that some huge financial companies in the United States were not financially sound.

The government stepped in to help. When the investment bank Bear Stearns was about to go under, the government

After the stock market crash of 1929, many investors were financially ruined and forced to sell their possessions at a loss in order to raise money.

organized a deal for another company to buy it, but at a value far below what it had been worth. Soon another investment bank, Lehman Brothers, was in trouble. This time, the government did not step in and allowed it to fail. Unfortunately, this made even more people lose faith in the markets.

It got to the point where the government believed the country's entire financial system was on the brink of collapse. If that happened, it could harm other parts of the national economy, as well as the global economy. The potential consequences were so dire that Congress voted for an enormous bailout. It authorized more than $700 billion of government money to help the struggling companies.

Since that event, many people have studied what happened to make things go so wrong. There is no single cause. Instead, it was a combination of poor business decisions on the part of the financial companies, as well as a lack of regulation from government agencies that could have helped prevent it.

LIGHTS OUT

In 2000 and 2001, California residents experienced a severe shortage of electricity. Blackouts occurred across the state. A number of things contributed to the shortage. Weather was one. There had not been much rain, which meant that electricity that was produced with hydroelectric power (water) became more scarce and more expensive. In addition, some energy companies were shutting down

power plants that made the electricity. This drove the prices even higher.

In this market, the energy companies sold electricity to public utility companies at one price, called the wholesale price.

Some workers did their jobs by flashlight in the early 2000s in California. The supply of electricity could not meet the demand, and blackouts occurred across the state.

Then, the utility companies sold the power to California citizens at a higher price, the retail price, so that they could make a profit. In order for the utility companies to make money—or at least break even—the retail price had to be higher than the wholesale price.

What happened, however, was that it became more expensive for the utility companies to buy the electricity, but the amount they sold it for stayed the same. Why? The utility companies were prohibited by law—that is, the government—to charge more than a certain amount to customers.

Getting in the Game

Being part of a market economy usually helps countries and individuals be more prosperous. However, it's often a challenge to break in. In the 1960s, the United States was giving India large amounts of wheat to help feed people. An Indian economist asked the United States to stop the donations. He thought India was so dependent on the shipments that its people were not learning how to grow their own wheat to feed themselves. Over time, the United States did cut back, and India developed its own wheat industry.

Sometimes, however, emerging markets do need a little help. The World Food Programme is an organization that helps fight hunger across the world. Through a program called Purchase for Progress, it helps connect small farmers in poor countries like Ethiopia and Uganda to larger markets. This gives the farmers incentive to grow surplus crops and then sell them for more profit.

Because prices did not go up, consumers had no incentive to use less energy. Demand quickly outpaced supply, and blackouts occurred when the supply dried up. Some of the public utility companies went bankrupt because they had to purchase electricity for more than they were legally allowed to sell it for.

The crisis got so bad that finally California's governor intervened. He authorized the state to pay for electricity that the utility companies could no longer afford. In the end, consumers did end up paying for the electricity—but through taxes, rather than by directly purchasing it.

China's Influence

Chinese economic reforms have led to a better standard of living for many Chinese people. They now have more income than in the past. Also, they have access to more open markets that encourage trade with foreign countries. As a result, Chinese citizens are getting used to having more stuff. Because of its huge population, the choices Chinese people make are having an impact on the rest of the world. The things they want are starting to affect what kinds of products companies are making. For example, the Buick is an American car that sells well in China. Certain design changes were made to make it even more appealing to Chinese buyers. These changes then were introduced to American models. Also, all these cars mean that the demand for commodities such as steel and oil has gone up. There are negative impacts as well. With its increased demand for energy, China has become a major producer of greenhouse gases that harm the environment.

MAKING THE SWITCH

A few decades ago, China and the Soviet Union were two of the world's largest countries. Both had communist governments and operated under command economies. Their governments set prices and decided who should do what. That began

In the mid-1980s, Soviet Union leader Mikhail Gorbachev intro-duced a series of economic reforms, but real economic progress did not occur until after the downfall of the Soviet Union in 1991.

to change in the late 1970s, when China introduced a series of changes to its economic system. In a move to a capitalist economy, the government began to encourage individuals to form private businesses. In addition, the government allowed more international trade and let foreign companies invest in Chinese businesses. China was able to export more, helping raise the stan-

dard of living for many Chinese people. Later, the Chinese government began a gradual change to let the market—instead of the government—determine prices.

At first, improvements to the Chinese economy had a lot to do with extra money coming into the country. However, China also improved its productivity, and workers became more efficient. This also contributed to the country's huge growth in the 1980s.

The Soviet Union also tried to improve its economy starting in 1985. Soviet leader Mikhail Gorbachev introduced the idea of *perestroika*, the Russian word for economic reforms. Things did not go as smoothly in the Soviet Union, however. The changes were not big enough, or fast enough, to change the whole system. The economy actually got worse. By the early 1990s, it had completely fallen apart. The economic disaster contributed to the fall of the Soviet Union in 1991, when the country broke up into fifteen separate nations. Without the old political barriers, market economies finally started to take hold in these new countries.

One of the nations was Estonia. Its new government set a determined path to convert to a market economy. It encouraged people and businesses to be entrepreneurs, cut back on rules and regulations, and made sure that private property was protected. In about a decade, Estonia had gone from being a poor country to a successful one.

Changing from a command economy to a market economy can be a difficult process. However, the system has demonstrated that it can offer more choices and provide better standards of living for people. Markets are not controlled from the top down by a government. Instead, they are the result of whatever the participants choose to do. In a small way, everyone's decisions are determined by what everyone else does. They also affect what everyone else does. Markets are constantly changing as cooperation and competition go hand-in-hand. The biggest products of a market economy are not cars or computers, but options and opportunities.

GLOSSARY

barter To trade two or more items directly, without involving money.

bond A type of loan taken out by a government and funded by many people.

capital The money or resources that are invested in a business.

commodity A basic material that does not change in value depending on who produces it.

economy of scale Having reduced production costs as a result of increased volume.

embargo The prohibition of trade with a country.

emerging market A nation with a quickly growing economy.

equilibrium A state of being in balance.

incentive A reason to do something.

interest Extra money charged on a loan.

market clearing price The price an item takes in order to keep supply and demand in balance.

mercantilism A philosophy that favors supporting only a country's domestic economy.

monopoly A complete domination of a product or industry by one company.

mortgage A loan taken out to buy real property, such as a house or land.

niche A specific part of something larger.

quota A fixed amount of something that must not be exceeded.

regulate To impose laws or rules on how companies or industries can do business.

standard of living The level of economic comfort someone has.

stock The capital in a company, available for investors to buy in shares.

subsidy A type of financial help, such as a cash payment.

surplus The extra amount of something beyond what is needed in the market.

tariff A tax imposed on imported products.

trade deficit A condition that occurs when a country's imports exceed its exports.

FOR MORE INFORMATION

Canadian Foundation for Economic Education (CFEE)
110 Eglinton Avenue West, Suite 201
Toronto, ON M4R 1A3
Canada
(416) 968-2236
Web site: http://www.cfee.org
The CFEE is a nonprofit organization that works to promote
    the economic capabilities and skills of Canadians by
    working in areas such as research, curriculum
    development, and strategic planning.

Center for International Private Enterprise (CIPE)
    Development Institute
1155 15th Street NW, Suite 700
Washington, DC 20005
(202) 721-9200
Web site: http://www.developmentinstitute.org
The CIPE's Development Institute is a program that helps
    students understand how democracy and market systems
    work together in economic development.

Council for Economic Education
122 East 42nd Street, Suite 2600
New York, NY 10168

(212) 730-7007 or (800) 338-1192

Web site: http://www.councilforeconed.org

The Council for Economic Education works to provide
economic and financial education to schools in the
United States and around the world.

Foundation for Teaching Economics (FTE)

260 Russell Boulevard, Suite B

Davis, CA 95616

(530) 757-4630

Web site: http://www.fte.org

The FTE works with students and teachers to examine
national and international issues related to the
economy.

Industry Canada

C. D. Howe Building

235 Queen Street

Ottawa, ON K1A 0H5

Canada

(613) 954-5031

Web site: http://www.ic.gc.ca

Industry Canada is a government department that works to
improve Canada's global economic position through
goals such as encouraging innovation and promoting
investment and fair trade.

International Trade Administration

U.S. Department of Commerce

1401 Constitution Avenue NW

Washington, DC 20230

(800) 872-8723
Web site: http://www.trade.gov
This government agency promotes U.S. business interests by
    encouraging trade and investment, and enforcing trade
    laws and agreements.

NYSE Euronext
11 Wall Street
New York, NY 10005
(212) 656-3000
Web site: http://www.nyse.com
NYSE Euronext is a major stock exchange encompassing
    markets throughout the United States and Europe.

WEB SITES

Due to the changing nature of Internet links, Rosen Publishing
has developed an online list of Web sites related to the subject
of this book. This site is updated regularly. Please use this link
to access the list:

http://www.rosenlinks.com/rwe/mark

FOR FURTHER READING

Andrews, David. *Business Without Borders*. Chicago, IL: Heinemann-Raintree, 2010.

Bezdecheck, Bethany. *Bailout!: Government Intervention in Business*. New York, NY: Rosen Publishing, 2010.

Crain, Cynthia D., and Dwight R. Lee. *Adam Smith*. Greensboro, NC: Morgan Reynolds Publishing, 2009.

Downing, David. *Capitalism*. Chicago, IL: Heinemann Library, 2007.

Fuller, Donna Jo. *The Stock Market*. Minneapolis, MN: Lerner Classroom, 2006.

Furgang, Kathy. *How the Stock Market Works*. New York, NY: Rosen Publishing, 2010.

Hamilton, Jill. *The U.S. Economy*. Farmington Hills, MI: Greenhaven Press, 2010.

Healey, Aaron. *Making the Trade*. Chicago, IL: Heinemann-Raintree, 2010.

Hollander, Barbara. *Booms, Bubbles, and Busts: The Economic Cycle*. Chicago, IL: Heinemann-Raintree, 2010.

Paulsen, Gary. *Lawn Boy*. New York, NY: Wendy Lamb Books, 2007.

BIBLIOGRAPHY

Cassidy, John. *How Markets Fail: The Logic of Economic Calamities*. New York, NY: Farrar, Straus and Giroux, 2009.

Economic Conversation. "The Invisible Hand: How Markets Work." Retrieved January 8, 2011 (http://www. theeconomicconversation.com/book/ch3.php).

Gerth, Karl. *As China Goes, So Goes the World: How Chinese Consumers Are Transforming Everything*. New York, NY: Hill and Wang, 2010.

Groz, Marc M. *Forbes Guide to the Markets*. Hoboken, NJ: John Wiley & Sons, 2009.

Hovey, Craig, and Gregory Rehmke. *The Complete Idiot's Guide to Global Economics*. New York, NY: Alpha Books, 2008.

Investopedia.com. "Market Failure." Retrieved January 8, 2011 (http://www.investopedia.com/terms/m/ marketfailure.asp).

McGregor, Richard. "Take the Back Seat: On Chinese Consumerism." *Nation*, December 27, 2010. Retrieved January 18, 2011 (http://www.thenation.com/article/ 156994/take-back-seat-chinese-consumerism).

Rabbior, Gary. "How Markets and Currencies Work." *Globe and Mail*, January 19, 2010. Retrieved January 6, 2011 (http://www.theglobeandmail.com/globe-investor/ investor-education/how-markets-and-currencies-work/ article1431020).

Read, Leonard. "I, Pencil." Irvington-on-Hudson, NY: Foundation for Economic Education (reprint), 2008. Retrieved January 19, 2011 (http://www.fee.org/pdf/ books/I,%20Pencil%202006.pdf).

Schuman, Michael. "Is the iPhone Bad for the American Economy?" Time.com, January 11, 2011. Retrieved January 15, 2011 (http://curiouscapitalist.blogs.time. com/2011/01/11/is-the-iphone-bad-for-the- american-economy).

Sowell, Thomas. *Applied Economics: Thinking Beyond Stage One.* Cambridge, MA: Basic Books, 2004.

Sowell, Thomas. *Basic Economics: A Common Sense Guide to the Economy.* Cambridge, MA: Basic Books, 2007.

Van Agtmael, Antoine. *The Emerging Markets Century.* New York, NY: Free Press, 2007.

World Food Programme. "P4P Overview." Retrieved January 8, 2011 (http://www.wfp.org/node/18711).

INDEX

About the Author

Diane Bailey writes on a variety of nonfiction topics for children and young adults. She lives with her two sons and two dogs in Kansas, where they consume a lot of stuff.

Photo Credits

Cover (top, banner), p. 1 © www.istockphoto.com/Lilli Day; cover (bottom) Ramin Talaie/Getty Images; pp. 8,17, 27, 34–35, 38, 49, 60 Mario Tama/Getty Images; p. 6 Miguel Villagran/Getty Images; p. 9 Saul Loeb/AFP/Getty Images; p. 11 © Charlie Neuman/The San Diego Union-Tribune/Zuma Press; p. 13 Jin Lee/Bloomberg via Getty Images; p. 15 Mark Hirsch/Bloomberg via Getty Images; p. 18 Shutterstock.com; pp. 20–21 Brand X Pictures/Thinstock.com; p. 24 JB Reed/Bloomberg via Getty Images; pp. 28–29 Jeff J Mitchell/Getty Images; pp. 30–31 Bradley Bower/Bloomberg via Getty Images; p. 33 © Cultura Limited/SuperStock; pp. 40–41 Findlay Kember/AFP/Getty Images; pp. 42–43 Keystone/Getty Images; pp. 46–47 Photos.com/Thinkstock.com; pp. 50–51 Comstock/Thinkstock.com; pp. 54–55 Lifesize/Thinkstock.com; pp. 56–57 Morris Engel/Getty Images; pp. 61, 66–67 Popperfoto/Getty Images; pp. 62–63 David McNew/Newsmakers/Getty Images; cover and interior graphic elements © www.istockphoto.com/Andrey Prokhorov; (back cover and interior pages) © www.istockphoto.com/Dean Turner; © www.istockphoto.com/Darja Tokranova (p. 26); www.istockphoto.com/articular (p. 59); © www.istockphoto.com/studiovision (pp. 69, 71, 74, 75, 77); © www.istockphoto.com/Chan Fu Soh (multiple interior pages).

Designer: Nicole Russo; Editor: Bethany Bryan;
Photo Researcher: Amy Feinberg